Original title:
I Came, I Thawed, I Conquered

Copyright © 2024 Creative Arts Management OÜ
All rights reserved.

Author: Elias Montgomery
ISBN HARDBACK: 978-9916-94-296-3
ISBN PAPERBACK: 978-9916-94-297-0

Ascension from a Frozen Past

In the land of ice, I did slip,
Whirling like a snowman, lost my grip.
Fingers turned numb, nose like a kite,
Taming the cold, a comical fight.

With snowflakes dancing, I took a leap,
Falling to the ground, my pride so steep.
Laughing at penguins, what a sight!
Wobbling about, I was pure delight.

Sunshine arrived, bringing forth cheers,
Melting my worries, along with my fears.
The thaw brought giggles, ice cubes in tow,
I splashed in puddles, letting joy flow.

Embracing the warmth, I spun like a top,
Slips turned to trips, no reason to stop.
From frozen to fun, a witty applause,
In this frosty realm, I found my cause.

Defiance of the Frozen Stillness

In a land where ice held sway,
I slipped and skidded my own way.
Snowflakes chuckled at my plight,
I danced like penguins in their flight.

With every stumble, laughter grew,
My frozen heart said, 'Let me through!'
Icicles laughed, they thought it gay,
But I had tricks, oh yes, hooray!

Seeds of Hope Bursting Forth

From frostbitten buds, green dreams awake,
Braving the chill, it's time to shake.
Out pops a sprout with a joyful grin,
Saying, 'Hey world, let the fun begin!'

In a garden where snowflakes used to dance,
Little green hearts are ready to prance.
Teachers of bloom, with quips and delight,
Wiggling and jiggling, spring's in our sight!

The Warmth of a Renewed Spirit

Through the frosty air, a giggle floats,
Hot cocoa dreams in fuzzy coats.
Laughter bubbles, like a warm surprise,
Melting the winter with happy sighs.

Oh, the cozy couch whispers my name,
While blankets laugh, it's all a game.
Sipping joy like it's a sweet treat,
In this fuzzy warmth, I'm feeling complete!

Awakening the Inner Flame

From the ashes of cold, a fire does leap,
With warm marshmallow dreams, I make a heap.
Roasting old worries, letting them go,
Licking the sweetness, don't be too slow!

Flames crackle jokes, in the chilly night air,
Determined to shine bright, as if we don't care.
In twinkling sparks, there's laughter to share,
A party of warmth in the crisp evening glare!

Flares of Strength in a Winter's Grip

Snowmen dance, they twist and twirl,
With floppy hats and arms that swirl.
A snowball fight, oh, what a blast,
But slipping 'round, I fell at last.

Hot cocoa spills, my shirt is stained,
While winter's chill has me maimed.
Yet laughter rings through frozen air,
As icicles dangle without a care.

Unraveling Chains of Ice

Tripped on ice, oh what a sight,
Like Bambi on skates, pure delight.
A dog went flying past my toes,
He laughed and barked, as winter froze.

With mittens warm, I will not cry,
Even as frozen dreams run dry.
An avalanche of giggles near,
Who knew that snow could bring such cheer?

Echoes of a Thawing Resolve

Once a statue, cold as stone,
Now a puddle, all alone.
The sun peeks in, does its best,
To make this icy world a jest.

Melting worries on my face,
Like drips of warmth, a rapid race.
Snowflakes dance, they slip and glide,
While I just wish for summer's ride.

From Snowdrifts to Sunlit Peaks

Climbing hills so white and steep,
With every step, I almost leap.
But gravity's humor knows no bounds,
As I tumble, laughter resounds.

Hot sun beams down, the snow melts fast,
Swimsuits soon, winter won't last.
From snowdrifts high to sunny shores,
I'll pack my fun and then explore.

Spring Songs from the Heart

Winter snores beneath the quilt,
Sunshine tickles, warmth is built.
Flowers giggle as they bloom,
Chasing off that frosty gloom.

Birds are chirping playful tunes,
Dancing 'neath the laughing moons.
Bunnies hop with glee and zest,
Springtime's here — we are so blessed!

From Ice to Radiance

Once a snowman, stiff and cold,
Now I'm free, so bright and bold!
Melting worries, watch them flee,
Sun-kissed joy, just let it be.

Chilling days are left behind,
What a quirky fate I find!
With a smile that warms the air,
I'm the sunshine, bright and rare!

The Triumph of Thawed Inmost

From frigid lands to sunny shores,
I've traded frowns for open doors.
The world is giggling, can't you see?
Dance it out, come join with me!

Ice cream drips, and laughter flies,
Melting hearts and tender sighs.
Frosty vibes now seem so far,
Grab your coat! Let's raise the bar!

Shadows Giving Way to Vibrance

Once a shadow, cold and gray,
Now I bask, come join the play!
Petals prance, and bees take flight,
All is funny, all feels bright!

Clouds have giggled, skies turned blue,
Lattes steaming, let's have two!
With sunshine in each silly beat,
Life's a laugh, oh, isn't it sweet?

Navigating the Thawing Tide

In winter's grip, I slipped and fell,
Like an ice cube lost, oh what the hell!
The sun shone bright, my chill parade,
Melted all fears in the frosty glade.

Penguins laughed as I skidded past,
A wobbly dance, what a silly cast!
With snowflakes giggling, I took a dive,
In this strange thaw, I'm very much alive!

Warm Winds of Change

A breeze rolled in, tickled my nose,
Swept through my boots, with a splash of prose.
Chattering squirrels set the scene,
As I tried to dance like a graceful queen.

The snowflakes cheered, flaked from above,
While I twirled around like I was in love.
With each silly sway, I lost my stride,
But oh what a mess in the joyful ride!

Journey Through the Frosted Veil

Through icy paths, my journey led,
With frosted whispers, I cautiously tread.
Laughter echoed from snowman foes,
Who mocked my waddle in winter clothes.

Each misstep, a comedic flair,
Frosty giggles filled the air.
Though I stumbled, I found my groove,
In the frosty veil, I started to move!

Eclipsing Doubt with Radiant Resolve

The sun peeked out, with a wink so sly,
Chased away doubts, made me laugh and cry.
I donned my cape made of bold sunlight,
Flew through the frost like a whimsical kite.

With every giggle, the ice slipped away,
Dancing with snowflakes, come what may!
A conqueror's spirit in laughter's embrace,
In this frozen realm, I found my place!

The Bloom Beyond Winter's Hold

Beneath the snow, a flower grins,
It jiggles in the sun's soft spins.
With frostbite kisses, it shakes away,
Saying, "I'm too cute to stay at bay!"

A tulip dressed in colors bright,
Dances with joy, what a delight!
Snowmen frown as blooms arise,
Their chilly faces full of surprise.

From Frostbitten to Flourishing

Once wrapped in blankets, cold and shy,
A zany daisy learned to fly.
"It's time for sunshine, no more chill,
I'm ready to bloom, oh what a thrill!"

With every drip from melting ice,
The world spins round, a bit of spice.
The garden laughs, it's quite a scene,
As bored snowflakes dodge the green.

Resurgence in Radiant Warmth

A sleepy seed under soil's hug,
Feels warmth tickle like a cozy shrug.
It wiggles up, then strikes a pose,
"Look at me, I'm a leafy rose!"

The sun beams down, a golden stage,
While weeds cheer on with giddy rage.
The grass does a happy little jig,
In a world where winter's just too big.

Breaking the Chains of Winter

Chained by cold, a bud would pout,
While birds outside just danced about.
It plotted pranks with frozen flair,
To sneak a peek, the world to share!

With giggles loud and petals wide,
It burst through ice, no place to hide.
"Oh look," it laughed, "I've made a friend—
Is springtime here? It's time to spend!"

Waking the Nature Within

The snowman lost his cool today,
He slipped and fell, oh what a sway!
The trees are yawning, stretch and bend,
Even the flowers are ready to blend.

Birds shout, 'Time for a new scene!'
Squirrels scurry, oh so keen.
Nature giggles, shakes off frost,
In this game, no one is lost!

Liberation from Winter's Cloak

A penguin disco, it's quite a sight,
Dancing in the sun, oh what delight!
Scarves are tossed, hats take flight,
Winter's grip is sheer contrite.

Giddy grasshoppers plot and scheme,
In the warmth, they'll chase the dream.
Melting ice in the sun's warm glow,
Who knew cold could be such a show?

Eclipsing the Cold Solitude

A lonely icicle, feeling blue,
Cries, 'Warmth, where are you?'
But the sun's rays with laughter burst,
'Time for a party, thaw, no more thirst!'

The snowflakes join in with flair,
From drab to fab, they dance in the air.
Frosty faces now beam with glee,
Springtime shenanigans, oh so free!

The Light After the Long Dark

Buried beneath layers, the soil sighs,
Crickets awaken, oh how they rise!
The moon chuckles, feeling spry,
As the sun starts to peek, oh my, oh my!

Chickens are clucking, 'Hooray, it's here!'
Winter's end is finally near.
Furry creatures pop out to play,
Laughing at chilly ghosts that sway!

The Defiance of the Frozen Soul

In a fortress made of ice,
A snowman rolled the dice.
He grinned with frosty cheer,
While winter streamed a sneer.

His carrot nose stood proud,
As blizzards swirled like clouds.
But then came warmth, oh dear,
His dreams began to veer.

With a hop and a dance,
He caught the sun's bright glance.
A melting mess he'd be,
Yet funny as could see.

Now he wears a swimsuit,
And does a silly hoot.
A frozen soul set free,
In laughter's jubilee.

A Cascade of Thawing Dreams

Once my thoughts were like blocks,
Chilled and full of frosty socks.
But then a warm breeze blew in,
And chaos did begin.

All my dreams began to slide,
In a silly joyful ride.
Water splashed in wild streams,
Waking up my frozen dreams.

Oh, the puddles danced with glee,
As snowflakes sang in spree.
I wished for sunny days,
While ice cubes waved in praise.

Now I strut through sunshine's glow,
In a hat that steals the show.
From dreams of cold to fun,
My thawing race is won!

Radiance Birthed from Frigid Shadows

In shadows cold and dim,
Lurks a snowflake on a whim.
It chuckled at its plight,
Warming up to find some light.

With every ray that hit,
It did a little split.
"Why be grumpy and blue?
When there's laughter to pursue!"

Oh, the frost began to flake,
As it did a happy shake.
Creating gleeful showers,
A carnival of thawing flowers.

Droplets danced in twirling joy,
Silly like a playful boy.
Under sunny skies I found,
My frozen self unbound!

The Embrace of an Unexpected Sun

Once I feared the sun's embrace,
With its warmth, I lost my place.
But then I saw it grin wide,
And decided not to hide.

Arms held high, I said, "Oh no!"
As the heat began to flow.
Sweating bullets in delight,
Melting slow, what a sight!

With chill no longer here,
I danced, kicked up some cheer.
Snowflakes laughed, all in fun,
As we basked beneath the sun.

No more winter's snoozy poise,
Just a chorus of noisy joys.
From frozen to a sunny run,
Life is better when it's fun!

A Story of Ice and Fire

Once a frozen block of fate,
Chillin' like a villain, it's too late.
Warm winds blew, and laughter roared,
Ice cream for thoughts, I was adored.

Laughter slipped, like snow in spring,
Frosty feelings began to sing.
I navigated through the chilly tease,
Eager to frolic like a frozen breeze.

Unveiling the Thawing Truth

Behind the ice, a tale was spun,
Sparkles of sparkle, oh what fun!
Patchy warmth wrapped around my thoughts,
Witty jests, like spicy shots.

The truth emerged, like sun on snow,
Slippery puns started to flow.
Jokes would slip and slide right past,
A thawing heart, surprised and fast.

Awakening the Frozen Heart

In a glacier realm, where giggles freeze,
Laughter echoing like a winter breeze.
Snowflakes danced, with whimsy bright,
Frozen hearts took flight, what a sight!

With every chuckle, the frost would melt,
Warmed by humor, joy was felt.
Dancing around, in a silly daze,
My heart thawed out in a frosty haze.

Melting Barriers of the Soul

Beneath the chill, my zest did freeze,
Cracking codes, with goofy keys.
With warm embraces, the ice took flight,
Swapping dull moods for pure delight.

Just like a sunbeam on an icicle's tip,
Giggles trickled, a joyful drip.
Breaking the walls with frosty glee,
Silly heartbeats, setting me free.

Flourishing Amidst Snowflakes

Snowflakes tickle my nose,
As I dance with clumsy toes.
My cheeks are rosy, quite absurd,
I'm the winter's goofy bird.

With hot cocoa in my hand,
Slipping on ice, what a grand stand!
Laughing at my frosty fate,
As penguins cheer, isn't it great?

Transcending the Cold Chains

Chained by mittens, I break free,
Wobbling like a bumblebee.
The frosty air tickles my brain,
My laughter's loud, but who's to blame?

Snowmen wink with carrot noses,
While I trip over winter poses.
Ice can't hold my zest for fun,
I'll slide and glide until I'm done!

Erupting from the Frosty Silence

In a world of white and cold,
I burst forth, brave and bold.
Snowballs fly, a cheeky plot,
I'm the warmth in winter's knot.

Through the silence, giggles spread,
As I tumble, fall, then tread.
Frosty fun, a joyful spree,
Winter's my stage, come watch me!

Light Shattering the Icebound Night

Moonlight glimmers on the frost,
As I prance, feeling like a boss.
With every slip, my spirit soars,
In this icy land, who needs doors?

Laughter echoes through the chill,
My heart races, what a thrill!
Cold can't freeze this happy dance,
So join me now, let's take a chance!

Beyond the Frostbound Existence

In the land where the snowflakes dance,
A penguin lost his chance for romance.
He slipped on ice with a clumsy charm,
Waved a wing, disarmed by his own alarm.

Beneath the chill in the frozen air,
Frosty lovers hide their despair.
They play peekaboo behind icy stalls,
Caught in a blizzard of frosty falls.

But then the sun beams with all its might,
Suddenly, snowmen take flight!
With carrot noses, they start to groove,
A frosty party—it's quite the move!

Laughter echoes through the bright thaw,
As igloos collapse with a silly flaw.
With every smile, winter's grip does ease,
And everyone's tinged with giggling freeze!

Transitions of the Yearning Heart

The groundhog peeks with a goofy grin,
He checks the weather with a sip of gin.
"Oh, spring is coming!" he gives a shout,
Then trips on grass—oh, what a clout!

Buds bloom bright, but bees start to tease,
Chasing folks around with silly wheeze.
A butterfly lands on my warm nose,
Guessing spring's here with a silly pose!

As flowers flirt in a colorful spree,
I dance with daisies—a sight to see!
We sway to a tune created by bees,
And laugh at winter's apologies with ease.

Frogs in the pond practice their croaky songs,
While silly squirrels engage in their prongs.
Love's in the air, and also some dirt,
For life is a comedy, not just a flirt!

The Sound of Melting Dreams

Icicles drip with a cartoonish plop,
As winter's grip begins to flop.
A snowman sneezes, then starts to weep,
His carrot nose falls! Oh, what a heap!

Puddles form with a splishy splash,
While ducks in the park start making a dash.
They quack with glee, in a water ballet,
A dance of delight in the warm new day.

The sun's warm grin turns frost into glee,
Melting my worries, setting me free.
With every drip, laughter fills the space,
As winter's chill runs a comedic race.

Snowflakes hold a farewell parade,
Leaving behind a sunlit charade.
Dreams of summer begin their ascent,
As we shake off the cold, feeling content!

Shadows Retreating Before the Light

As shadows flee from the morning sun,
They bump into walls, oh what fun!
Shrieking and squeaking, they jostle in fright,
Trying to escape from the warm, bold light.

Socks in the dryer compete for a laugh,
Playing hide-and-seek in their silly craft.
The lost ones grumble, calling for peers,
While sunlight bursts, dissolving their fears.

Cupcakes rise, with candy on top,
While shadows stumble and flip, then flop.
They mimic dance moves, not quite in time,
Creating a rhythm that's simply sublime!

Sunny days bring their awkward retreat,
While shadows march to a quirky beat.
With every giggle, the world comes alive,
As whimsy and warmth take a fun dive!

Triumph Over Frigid Horizons

A penguin wobbles, slips with glee,
In socks that don't quite fit his feet.
He aims to surf on melting ice,
But lands with flair, not once, but twice.

Snowflakes giggle, whispering tales,
Of icebergs melting, ships with sails.
With every slip, he claims a cheer,
His hopes raised high, his courage clear.

He scoffs at winter, shaking his fist,
As sunshine peeks through fog and mist.
The dance of thaw calls, what a show,
With every slip, he steals the glow.

A frosty world in giggles shrouds,
While laughter bursts from frozen clouds.
With passion bold, no chill remains,
Our silly hero warms the plains.

Regrowth After the Frost

Under snowmen who stand so tall,
A brave little sprout dares to sprawl.
With a wink and a wiggle, it starts to grow,
Chasing away winter's hoarfrost throes.

The daisies peek from beneath the drape,
In their sunny hats, no need to scrape.
They elbow the snow with a petal's nudge,
Declaring spring with a jovial grudge.

Squirrels giggle as they work to stash,
Nuts in the thaw, in a madcap dash.
But slips and flops bring such delight,
As acorn bombs soar into the light.

In this frosty park where laughter blooms,
Joy takes root in the warm afternoons.
With every thaw, the silly blooms thrive,
Oh, the fun in the effort to survive!

Breakthrough of the Sunlight Dream

Sunbeams burst through frosty panes,
While penguins plot with whimsical brains.
They form a squad with laughter loud,
To conquer winter, daring and proud.

A snowball fight ensues, no doubt,
With fluffed-up coats, they glide about.
Each throw a giggle, each slip a cheer,
In this sunshine dream, winter's end is near.

The clouds shed tears, not of despair,
But from laughter shared in the warm spring air.
With every ray that lands on cheeks,
The victory of warmth is what one seeks.

As the frost retreats, the world spins bright,
Dancing in daydreams from day to night.
The cheerful bands toast o'er hot cocoa,
To brightened futures, oh what a show!

The Dance of Deceiving Cold

Winter waltzes on ice-cold toes,
But a silly fox knows how it goes.
With a twirl and a leap, he dodges the freeze,
Laughing as snowflakes cling to his knees.

The trees wear frost like a sparkling dress,
While critters collide in their playful mess.
A blizzard howls, a tempest is bold,
Yet joy pops up like a mischief untold.

The icicles dangle, sharp and bright,
But the fox just grins, feeling delight.
He takes a tumble, slips on the ice,
What a foolish prince, but oh, so nice!

So as winter prances in crystal white,
Our furry friend dances with sheer delight.
For beneath thick blankets of snow and cold,
Warmth and laughter are treasures to hold.

The Flame Awakens

From frozen toes to wiggly dance,
I slipped on ice and took a chance.
With mittens tossed and scarf unwound,
My winter woes were nowhere found.

A snowman watched with a silly grin,
As I skated 'round with a cheeky spin.
My cocoa spilled, a chocolate shower,
Proving warmth can come with power.

The squirrels watched in awe and glee,
As I tripped and fell—not so gracefully.
But laughter echoed, spirits soared,
In this bright, zany, winter score.

So here's to heat, both near and far,
From ice-cold struggles to a blazing star.
Chasing the chill, embracing the fun,
Laughing out loud 'til the day is done.

Harnessing the Heat of Change

A chilly breeze meets my warm embrace,
In this tangled web of a whimsical race.
With enthusiasm dressed in fuzzy socks,
I take apart those winter blocks.

The sun peeked through my frosty dome,
And suddenly I felt quite at home.
Melting worries, well, what a thrill,
I'm on a roll, looking for the chill.

Pancakes flip in the steamy air,
My kitchen's now a great affair.
With syrup flows and laughter sails,
Watch out, world, as joy prevails!

And as I bask in sunlight's glow,
I find the humor in life's flow.
The ice may crack, but laughter stays,
Turning frost into sunny days.

Battling Through the Doldrums

On snowy days, I felt the strain,
Boredom wrestling with my brain.
But then I donned my hero cape,
And banished gloom with icy tape.

Hula hoops and snowball fights,
Became my tricks to spark delights.
With boots that squeaked like rubber ducks,
I battled frost, my hidden plucks.

The couch had beckoned, soft and warm,
But I chose fun over winter's charm.
A dance-off in my living room,
Eliminating that frozen gloom.

So call me brave, or call me bold,
I'll break the ice, story told.
With mirth and giggles, I will clown,
And turn this frown upside down.

Emersion into Gentle Warmth

The world was cold, a frosty place,
But I decided to find my grace.
With a silly hat and mismatched gloves,
I searched for giggles, embraced by love.

A sunbeam found me picking flowers,
Amongst the flakes and chilly showers.
A dance party for the snowflakes bright,
Even the clouds began to smile right.

From frozen fingers to toasty bites,
I warmed the air on those chilly nights.
With playful jests and friends so near,
We formed a circle, spreading cheer.

Riding the waves of laughter's tune,
The chilling days had turned to June.
With every joke, each friendly balm,
Winter's bite now felt quite calm.

The Warm Embrace of Resilience

In winter's cold grip, I stepped outside,
My breath a cloud in the frosty tide.
With each little slip on the icy ground,
I chuckled aloud, what joy I found.

Snowflakes danced down, a tickle fight,
My nose was red, what a comical sight.
Bundled like a marshmallow, I waddled around,
Laughing so hard, fell over, I frowned.

A snowman appeared, a jolly old chap,
With a carrot for a nose, he was quite the sap.
We had a chat on that chilly day,
But all he said was, "Just chill out, hey!"

Resilience wrapped me tight like a hug,
I embraced the cold, though it felt like a jug.
For laughter is warm, even when skies are gray,
A sunny heart conquers, come what may.

Awakening the Slumbering Essence

From under layers of blankets, I did rise,
With sleepy eyes, and a yawn that defies.
The frost on my window, a glittery play,
Whispered softly, 'Come dance in the fray.'

Socks mismatched, I stumbled in glee,
Caught my big toe on the coffee table's spree.
The floor was a dancefloor of sneakers and ice,
And I, the lead dancer, oh how nice!

Unruly hair just added to the flair,
With each brush through, it stood up in air.
I laughed at the mirror, a sight so absurd,
An ice sculpture alive, not a mere frozen bird.

Every giggle cracked the chilly air,
Breaking the silence, a joyful affair.
Resilience awoke, bright as a sunbeam,
In this winter wonderland, I dared to dream.

Journey Through the Frozen Veil

With boots too big, I marched through the snow,
A heroic quest, though my feet could not go.
I slipped and I slid, a cartoonish spree,
Waving my arms like a wild bumblebee.

The snowflakes giggled as they danced all around,
While I tried to walk without falling down.
Each step was a laugh, a slip, then a plop,
This journey's an adventure, where silly won't stop.

A snow fort I built, but it crumbled away,
Just like my plans for a cool winter play.
Yet laughter echoed, resilience so bright,
I threw snowballs at fate, with pure delight.

So let this be known, as I journeyed with cheer,
In the face of the ice, laughter's my spear.
Through frozen folds, my spirit ran free,
For fun is the key to true victory!

Defiant Against the Winter's Breath

The chill in the air tried to steal my smile,
But I wore a grin that stretched a good mile.
Woke up one day, dressed like a bear,
With mittens and scarves, oh, fashion so rare!

Out in the snow, I challenged the frost,
"Not today!" I yelled, "You won't be the boss!"
With each playful tumble, I showed my resolve,
Against winter's breath, a warrior to evolve.

As I rolled in the snow, my giggles rang clear,
Creating a winter kingdom, without any fear.
A snow angel I made, though it looked like a blob,
Still, joy in the frosty mess, I knew I'd win the mob.

So here's to the fun, with laughter my sword,
In battles with winter, my spirit's restored.
Through chilly resistance, I'll dance and I'll play,
With warmth in my heart, I'll seize the day!

A Heart That Sizzles

With a heart that's hot, like bacon on the fry,
I danced through the snow, oh my, oh my!
Chasing snowflakes, dodging a cold stare,
I turned winter's frost into bright summer air.

A frosty romance, just me and my coat,
But I lost my balance, flew off like a goat.
The snowmen laughed, they couldn't believe,
That my inner fire was hard to deceive.

Laughter erupted, in warm, melting tones,
I painted the world with my silly hormones.
Flipping pancakes, whilst catching some sun,
Who knew melting ice could be so much fun!

So let's heat the town, toast to the vibes,
With giggles and joy, let's forget winter jibes.
A heart that sizzles, a spirit so bright,
Turning winter's chill into sheer delight!

Rising from the Chilling Depths

Out from the frost, like a quirky old sprout,
With layers of ice, I just had to shout!
The cold tried to pin me, all snug and tight,
But I wriggled like jelly and danced in the light.

Penguins took notice, they stood in a row,
As I twirled and twisted, stealing the show.
With a shimmy and shake, I rose up with flair,
Who knew winter blues could lift off the chair?

I countered the freeze with a giggle and grin,
The icy depths knew they couldn't win.
So here's to the warmth, we'll throw a parade,
While snowflakes melt down, my plans never fade.

Conquered the cold, no frostbite in sight,
Found joy in the thaw, all day and all night.
With friends like the sun, let's play and be bold,
Rising from depths, feeling silly and sold!

The Steam of New Beginnings

In the kettle of life, I boiled with glee,
Steam rising up like a warm cup of tea.
With a pop and a hiss, emotions unfurled,
Who knew all it took was to rock the cold world?

Each bubble a promise, each splash a delight,
Caffeine-fueled antics, oh what a sight!
I brewed up some laughter, poured joy in a mug,
While winter was fuming, I gave it a shrug.

A pinch of adventure, a dash of surprise,
From frosty foundations, I cropped winter lies.
With every fresh moment, I crisped up the air,
The steam of new dreams blowing everywhere.

So let's crack some smiles, as we sip and we swirl,
With warmth in our hearts, let's take on the world.
As the kettle whistles in harmony and cheer,
I raise my cup high, the fun time is here!

Embracing the Thawing Sun

When the sun burst forth, it began a whole scene,
Melting away, my winter routine.
With a flip and a flop, I rolled in the rays,
Dancing with shadows in playful displays.

The ice cubes surrendered, they slid and they slipped,
As I bounced through puddles, hilariously tripped.
With warmth on my cheeks and laughter in tow,
I pranced through the streets, stealing the show.

The flowers all giggled, they dressed up in bloom,
While critters joined in, dispelling the gloom.
Showing off colors that glitter like fun,
Embracing this spring, oh, what a run!

So here's to the thaw, let's bask in our glee,
A party of warmth, just goofy and free.
With a chuckle and jig, let's welcome the sun,
In this wacky thawing, we've only just begun!

The Dawn After Winter's Veil

Winter jeans almost fit me tight,
But spring comes with a dance so light.
Snowmen get the fluffiest hair,
As sun beams cheer from everywhere.

Birds tweet tunes in a cheeky tune,
While ice cubes melt by the afternoon.
The coffee's hot but don't forget,
Last night's chill is hard to regret.

Buds pop out in a joyful spree,
Even my nose wants to run free.
Smiling at the frozen past,
I chuckle, wondering how long it'll last.

With every flower that starts to bloom,
I shed away my winter gloom.
So here we are, spring hugs in sight,
Thanks for the laughs, winter's delight!

Uprising of the Warmth

Socks and sandals in a bold parade,
A fashion statement, I just made!
Flip-flops echo a comical cheer,
While winter boots are left in fear.

Sunshine splashes like paint on the wall,
Sneezy humans start to sprawl.
Sunglasses on, looking so cool,
As laughter echoes through the school.

Picnics spring forth from kitchens wide,
With sandwiches that we can't quite hide.
The ants march in with a tiny song,
We wave goodbye to winter long.

The warmth arrives, it's quite absurd,
As trees wear their leaves like they're 'preferred.'
Let's raise a toast to the melting feel,
For all things silly make spring so real!

Human Spirit Breaking Free

Lock up your mittens, it's time to play,
Freezing troubles melt away!
Laughter bubbles in sun's embrace,
No more hiding in winter's case.

Sweaters tossed like confetti bright,
Ice-cube chases just feel so right.
We wear our joy like a badge of fun,
Leaving behind the icy run.

Frogs start croaking with glee and might,
Joined by bunnies in delight!
No more chills, just sunny spells,
In this charming, funny realm of wells.

Here's to the spirit of laughs so free,
Dancing in rhythms of jubilee.
Goodbye to frost, hello to glee,
Our hearts in unison, oh can you see?

Shedding Layers of Frigid Pain

Peeling off layers like an onion's gift,
What's this warmth? A comical lift!
No more thermal hugs around my waist,
My belly's giggles can now be faced.

Hot cocoa's gone, it's lemonade now,
Replaced with smiles, take a bow!
The fireplace whispers a smoky tune,
While outside blooms the sunny June.

Crisp air hugs all, like friends unite,
As flip-flops dance through the light.
We strut our stuff with jiggly glee,
For winter's gone, and we are free!

So here's to the thaw and laughter bright,
With long lost sunbeams shining light.
Let's toast to warmth and silly play,
For winter's chill has lost its sway!

Rise of the Spring Spirit

Once a chill, I was so cool,
Now I'm here to break the rule.
Snowmen shiver, they can't fit,
As I dance and throw a hit.

Birds on branches start to sing,
While I whirl and do my thing.
Ice-cream trucks are on the way,
Turning winter into play.

With a twirl I warm the breeze,
Bubbles float and kiss the trees.
Snowflakes melt as I parade,
Sunshine blossoms in the glade.

So bring your shorts, it's time to cheer,
The snowman's gone, so never fear!
With laughter echoing this spring,
Let's celebrate the joy I bring!

From Ice to Ember

Frosty mornings long have passed,
Sunshine breaks, oh, what a blast!
Chillin' out is now a feat,
Warming up with tasty heat.

Candles flicker, hearts ignite,
Once so frigid, now so bright.
Falling ice with a goofy slip,
Sudden warmth, I take a trip.

Who needs snow when you've got fun?
Sunscreen on? Oh yes, I'm done!
Mittens gone, it's party time,
I'm the reason for the rhyme.

Laughing loud with friends around,
From icy ground to joy unbound.
Celebrate this sassy shift,
As cool turns hot, oh what a gift!

Unveiling the Warmth Within

Underneath that frozen shell,
Lies a spirit that can yell!
Winter games? Oh what a bore!
Watch me dance and start to roar!

Layers peel like a big onion,
Chilly vibes, I'm not a pun-tion.
Throw your scarf, let's shake some sillies,
Tickle toes, let's spread some thrillies.

Bonfire crackles, stories flow,
Laughing hard, just watch us glow.
No more shivers, only heat,
Together now, we beat the sleet.

Out of frost, into this blaze,
Here I shine for sunny days.
Life's a winter, then a feast,
With a giggle, we're released!

The Thaw of a Thousand Winters

Once I sat in icy gloom,
Now I burst out with a bloom!
Mittens tossed, it's time to cheer,
Snowflakes melting—bring the beer!

Ice cubes dance in playful sways,
Long-lost warmth in funny ways.
Giggling at the frost's demise,
Sipping cocoa as it fries.

No more chilling, just the fun,
Spring is here, it's time to run!
We'll paint the flowers, soft and sweet,
With squishy shoes upon our feet.

So here's a toast to shiny skies,
To giggles where the winter lies.
A thousand frosts now laid to rest,
Let's laugh and play, it's for the best!

Frozen Footprints on the Path of Change

Out in the cold, I slipped and slid,
My frozen toes were quite the bid.
Each step I took, a quirky dance,
Who knew ice could lead to a chance?

Snowball fights left me in stitches,
While frostbite laughed at my glitches.
But with each fall, a lesson learned,
In chilly chaos, my heart yearned.

With every slip, a giggle fits,
Life's ups and downs are big ol' hits.
So here I trot, with less of a care,
Marching on, with frosty flair.

So raise a mug of hot cocoa cheer,
For every fall draws friends near!
With frozen footprints and laughter so bright,
I journey on, in pure delight.

Melting Mirrors Reflecting Triumph

In a hall of glass, couldn't find my face,
A frosty figure, in a funny place.
Trying to shine but slipping away,
Who knew mirrors could play such a game?

Dripped down the wall, like a melted cheer,
"Reflects a winner!" the ice said, "Dear!"
With each sagging curve, I grinned and twirled,
Funny how triumph can soften the world.

I broke the ice, oh what a smash,
Turning my frown to a gleeful splash.
In puddles of laughter, I found my glow,
When chilly worries began to slow.

"Look at us now!" the mirrors exclaimed,
From frosty fumbles, the fire named.
In this melting game, our joy winds tight,
With every slip, we make things bright!

From Ice to Fire: A Journey Unbound

Frostbite bites, but I laugh it away,
Chasing the chill with each goofy sway.
Like a snowman who shed all his fluff,
I danced through winter, just having enough.

The warmth of spring peeked 'round the bend,
"Is it too soon?" I asked my friend.
But the sun shone bright, oh so slick,
Turns out thawing was quite the trick!

From icy grip to a fiery flip,
I swirled through seasons, with a sunny quip.
A snowball warrior turned summer's delight,
Who knew melted dreams could take flight?

So here's to the spring and to warmer days,
Where laughter blooms in magnificent ways.
What a ride from frozen to grand,
This journey unbound, so sweet and unplanned!

Beneath the Frost, a Heart Awakens

With frost on my nose and a smile so wide,
I ventured forth on this slippery ride.
Underneath layers, a warmth did ignite,
A heart once buried now danced in delight.

The cold tried to get me, but oh, what a jest,
I twirled on the ice, feeling truly blessed.
With every shiver, I giggled and spun,
Who knew chilly times could be so much fun?

Under the blanket of snowflakes so bright,
A heart's hidden rhythm began to ignite.
Joy bubbled up, like a hot choc'late stream,
Awakened and vibrant, I chased after dreams.

So let the frost come, let the winter play,
With each frozen moment, I'll find my way.
Beneath all the cold, I found my own tune,
Echoing warm laughs beneath the cold moon.

Embracing the Season of Renewal

In winter's chill, I donned my gear,
With mittens huge, I faced my fear.
A snowball launched, it missed the mark,
Instead, it hit a barking lark.

The sun peeks out, it's feeling bold,
But my hot tea has grown quite cold.
My nose is red, a comical sight,
Trying to dance in the fading light.

Children giggle, they whirl and sway,
While I trip over my own ballet.
The ice begins to melt away,
Surprising squirrels on their fray.

So here's to spring, let laughter sprout,
I'll twirl and spin; I'll strut about.
With a spring in step, the air's divine,
Our clumsy antics—perfectly fine.

Transcending the Frosted Horizon

Like frosty windows, I can see,
The world outside laughing at me.
With slipped on ice, my stance is weak,
A penguin's waddle? What a peak!

The horizon glows, a gleaming tease,
I'm cheered by chirps from busy bees.
Wrapped in layers, I look so grand,
Too much fabric! Can't lift my hand.

The thaw's a call, a playful song,
But my dance moves still feel quite wrong.
With puddles formed like little lakes,
I leap right in, whatever it takes!

Owls are hooting—"What a display!"
As I slide and pivot, my own ballet.
The frost tries hard to steal the show,
Yet warmth and giggles begin to grow.

Heartbeats Against the Cold

Crisp air bites, it makes me jump,
I shuffle forward, then take a thump.
My heart races like a racecar,
Yet I can't find my socks—what a star!

The wind whispers secrets that tease my face,
Every chattering tooth, a comical case.
But laughter erupts as I dash for the door,
A snowman standing guard, oh what a chore!

With every giggle, we gain some heat,
As we almost trip, while trying to fleet.
A winter party, oh how we strive,
With cocoa and friends, we come alive!

So here's to the cold, the thrill of the chase,
I swirl through the wind with a dorky grace.
Let's dance on the ice, our hearts a-twirl,
In the frosty fun, let laughter unfurl.

Stretching Toward the Sun's Embrace

With each sunny ray, I stretch and yawn,
My winter coat feels like an old prawn.
Out comes the hat with its frumpy flair,
A quest for warmth? I'll get there, I swear!

Flowers are waking, what a sight to see,
While I stumble past a buzzing bee.
The sun's a joker, it plays peek-a-boo,
And makes me dance like I'm just passing through.

I wave at the clouds, they giggle and sway,
As I trip on a branch, oh what a display!
With laughter, we burst, in a fit of cheer,
While ice cream cones wait for a sunny peer.

So to the sky, I lift my gaze,
In warming beams, I've lost my craze.
With every step toward the golden warmth,
I embrace this joy—so true and strong.

The Triumph of a Heart Reborn

Once a frozen block of ice,
Shivering at every toss and dice.
Laughter bubbled, made me sway,
A sunny joke brightened my day.

In a world of snowball fights,
I found my joy on frosty nights.
With every chuckle, away it fled,
Melting doubt, making room instead.

Now a heart that dances free,
Unfurling wings, oh joy, oh glee!
What once was cold, now shines so bright,
A rising star in frosty night.

So here's to fun and laughter loud,
Leaving behind a chilly shroud.
From frozen whispers to joyful shouts,
My heart reborn, no more doubts.

Waking the Slumbering Spirit

Oh sleepy soul, where have you been?
Hidden beneath a mountain of sin.
Time to shake off those frozen dreams,
And dance in sunlight's warming beams.

From hibernation, I'm breaking free,
Chuckling at how cold I used to be.
With each small step, I start to giggle,
It feels so good, I start to wiggle.

Old worries, like ice, begin to crack,
I'm marching forward, never looking back.
My spirit twirls in a summer breeze,
Sighing with joy—oh, such a tease!

Now let's throw a party, make it big,
Invite the warmth, do a happy jig.
What was once lost has found the way,
Risen like dough on a baking day.

A Dance Between Ice and Flame

Come gather 'round for a frosty show,
Where ice and flame put on a glow.
The frost tried hard to put me down,
But I just twirled in my warmest gown.

With each playful step on the slushy floor,
I laughed at ice, said, 'Give me more!'
Combining heat with a wink so sly,
I made the snowflakes flutter and fly.

So much sass in my little prance,
I spun with joy, an awkward dance.
Who knew the chill could spark such fun?
Here comes the sun; let's all outrun!

A giggle here, a shiver there,
The chilly air becomes a dare.
From icicles to the warmth of day,
It's a funny game; now, let's play!

Charting a Course through Chilly Waters

Set sail, you brave, frostbitten soul,
Through icy waves, we'll find control.
A map made of giggles, wind in our hair,
Adventures await, so let's prepare!

The morning sun whispers sweet delight,
As we navigate through the frosty night.
With joyous hearts, we row so free,
No iceberg's gonna stop you and me!

Dancing over waves, we'll splash and cheer,
Our frosty fears all disappear.
What was once bleak now sparkles bright,
Like glitters of frost in the warm sunlight.

So grab your oars, let's make a scene,
With laughter as loud as a well-oiled machine.
Together we'll conquer the chilly spree,
And paint the waters with glee, just you and me!

March of Rejuvenation

The sun peeks out, a sly little grin,
Winter's grip loosens, let the fun begin.
Pants soaked from puddles, shoes filled with glee,
Nature's sneak preview of spring's jubilee.

Bunnies bounce back, they're planning a race,
With snowmen crumbling, oh what a disgrace!
The flowers are laughing, daring to bloom,
While squirrels are planning a grand parade zoom!

Chickens break dance in a parking lot lot,
All spring's wild antics are hitting the spot.
A honking goose winks, it knows what's in store,
Prepare, dear world, it's spring—never a bore!

So grab all your shades, let's step to the beat,
Kick off winter socks, now isn't that sweet?
With laughter and sunshine, our spirits will soar,
March of rejuvenation—we're ready for more!

Invincible Against the Frost

Brr, it was cold, I was stuck in my chair,
Wrapped up like a sandwich, was quite the affair.
But thawing commenced, I declared with a grin,
With coffee as armor, let the thawing begin!

Frosty breath huffed, like a dragon at play,
But I'm warming up, what more can I say?
With hot cocoa powered, I laugh at the chill,
My socks mismatched, but I'm owning the thrill!

The icicles dangle like chandeliers bright,
I prance past the snow with a dance full of light.
With mittens like monsters, all fuzzy and bold,
I laugh at the winter—there's mischief to unfold!

So come on, dear winter, let's have a parade,
Invincible spirit, let's throw some confetti made.
With each step I take, I'll twirl through the frost,
With giggles and joy, so nothing is lost!

Awakening the Brilliance Within

From the depths of cold, a laughter awakes,
A shimmering sparkle, oh what a mistake!
My slippers are marching, socks starting to sing,
With coffee as fuel, I'm ready for spring!

Melting the ice, in my kitchen I dance,
The blender's a band—who needs second chance?
Eggs in a scramble, we're flipping with zest,
Whisking up dreams, it's a morning fest!

In parks where it's springing, the squirrels take flight,
They chatter in gossip, oh what a sight!
My wiggle and jiggle got all of them wild,
Awakening brilliance, I'm nature's own child!

So bring on the warmth, let the sunshine be bold,
With smiles and laughter, nothing feels old.
The brilliance inside us is ready to shine—
The world's our playground, all frosted divine!

Moving Beyond the Ice Cascade

With snowflakes a-drifting, I stumble and skid,
Laughing at weather's whimsical bid.
From ice block to puddle, my journey's a blast,
Each slip leads to giggles, oh how it goes fast!

The air is a canvas, the sun paints in gold,
As icy cascades bring stories untold.
I frolic with joy, my frosty friends cheer,
With each step I take, spring whispers to hear!

Wiggles of laughter, the flowers all peek,
As we bid adieu to these cold little streaks.
The birds hold a concert, a ruckus of cheer,
Moving beyond ice, the fun's drawing near!

So splash in the puddles, let's dance in the rain,
With sunshine as backdrop, let go of the chain!
From icy to lively, it's a bumpy old path,
But laughs on the way, oh, let's do the math!

Warmth Eclipses the Winter's Grasp

In frostbitten shoes, I take my stand,
A snowball in hand, oh isn't this grand?
The Chill's icy finger gives way to my cheer,
With laughter in pockets, no room for a sneer.

Hot cocoa flows like a river so sweet,
I dance in the snow, what a whimsical feat!
The snowmen are giggling, the penguins agree,
As warmth sweeps the land and sets winter free.

Frosty's nose, he says, misses the sun,
But here I am leaping, oh isn't this fun?
A blanket of laughter; the chill's out of style,
With cocoa mustaches, let's hang for a while.

So let the warm rays melt all the white fears,
I'll bring out the sunshine, let's chase off the tears!
What once was a blizzard, now chuckles and glee,
As warmth wraps the world, come join in with me!

Shattering Silence: A Resilient Roar

In a world of white whispers, I shout my delight,
With a snowman that giggles, we'll dance through the night!
The penguins are clapping, the squirrels in a whirl,
No more frozen frowns, let's give winter a twirl!

The icicles tremble, they sense my bold flair,
With a belly full of giggles, I'm light as the air.
The snowflakes are laughing, they tumble and sway,
As I launch my warm roar, chasing cold blues away.

The silence is shattered; hear echoes of glee,
A thaw in the air, let the fun run free!
With a wave of my hand, winter's grip shall cease,
In the circus of warmth, prepare for release!

No more muffled valleys, tune into this score,
As winter uncorks and trips on the floor!
With each hearty chuckle, we brighten the gray,
Together we'll giggle this frost away!

Embracing the Dawn of New Beginnings

With a sleepy-eyed yawn, I greet morning's glow,
The sun peeks in shyly, melting ice with a show.
Caffeine in my cup, I sip with a grin,
As winter's cold fingers start loosening their win.

The birds chirp a tune that tickles my feet,
As I wobble around, oh isn't spring neat?
With the frost giving way to much warmer fun,
The world spins in laughter, oh what a run!

In layers I shed like a cake on my plate,
My icy past gone, no longer I wait.
The buds start to bloom, a riot of cheer,
As I leap through the puddles, wiping away fear.

So come, join the party as daylight expands,
With humor and sunshine, versatility stands!
In this festival of warmth, let new tales be spun,
As winter surrenders, and laughter's begun!

Transformation in the Heart of Winter

In a land where the frosty air tickles my nose,
I step in a snowdrift and stumble—who knows?
With a twist and a tumble, I shake off the chill,
As warmth wiggles in, like a mischievous thrill.

A hat on my head, it barely fits right,
As I march through the blizzards, sharing my light.
The snowflakes start dancing, with glee in their flight,
While I waddle and giggle, all bundled up tight.

Winter's no match for my joyous parade,
As the squirrels chuckle at the splash that I made.
With boots full of jokes and a heart made of cheer,
I prance through the drifts, bringing warmth ever near.

So let's hoot and let's holler, the cold's here to stay,
But I'm ready with sunshine to brighten the way.
As winter transforms into giggles of fun,
Watch me melt all the ice with my heart's golden run!

When Cold Meets Courage

In a freezer of fears, I took a stand,
With ice cubes for armor, I made my plan.
Laughing at frostbite, I danced with a sigh,
Turning chilly confronts into a warm, bright sky.

The snowflakes fell down, I gave them a wink,
As icicles formed, I paused to think.
Should I march forward, or linger in doubt?
With each silly slip, I knew what life's about.

Frosty breath blowing like a wintery tune,
I juggled my courage beneath the cold moon.
Who knew that bravery would be such a blast?
While glaciers were grumpy, I had a snowball blast!

So here's to the chill that made me a laugh,
A frosty beginning, but oh, what a path.
With humor in heart, and laughter in mind,
I hugged the cold tight—what magic I'd find!

Awakening from a Crystal Slumber

From a snooze beneath frosty crystals I wake,
Stretching and yawning, oh, what a mistake!
A frozen pancake, I flip and I flop,
But the laughter erupts, and I just cannot stop.

The sun peeks in, saying, "Hey, let's thaw!"
With giggles and snorts, I roll on the floor.
Ice cream dreams vanish in rays of new light,
Who knew waking up could be such a delight?

I slip on a sock, but it slides down my leg,
'Twas my last bit of warmth, now I truly beg.
With slippers as weapons, and coffee in hand,
I chase off the chill, and make my bold stand.

Each glacier's a friend when you laugh with the sun,
A frosty old past can't keep me from fun.
So here's to the thaw, the warm, sunny cheer,
A crystal awakening—nothing to fear!

The Warmth of Unfrozen Aspirations

A melting ambition on a snowy path,
With visions of sunshine, I'm skipping the math.
Who needs a map when I'm laughing so loud?
Past frosty frustrations, I stand proud.

I reached for the stars, but slipped on a flake,
Did a twirl on the ice, oh, what a mistake!
Yet, giggles erupted from my glacial fall,
And soon I was bouncing, with dreams big and tall.

As the chill tried to hold me, I just grabbed a seat,
With warmth in my heart and frost-tipped feet.
I baked up a plan with some chocolate delight,
Even winter can't stop me from feeling just right!

So here's to our hopes, all unfrozen and bright,
Chasing sunny futures with giggles in flight.
While winter may frown, my spirit stays free,
With sarcasm and warmth, oh, what joy it can be!

Glacial Battles and Fiery Victories

In the arena of snow, I wield my bright spoon,
Defending my fortress beneath the full moon.
With marshmallow shields and a hot cocoa lance,
I waged a fierce war, but all I could do was dance.

The chilly front charged, but I scoffed and I joked,
Launching my cannon made of soft toasted yolk.
The snowmen all laughed, they'd never seen cheer,
In a battle of wit, I obliterate fear.

The war cry of ice met the heat of my grin,
As laughter erupted, the thaw would begin.
With snowball ammunition and giggles in tow,
I claimed fiery victories, oh, what a show!

So here's to the clashes where humor takes flight,
Frosty skirmishes spark laughter so bright.
In the dance of the glacial, I find my delight,
Winning with warmth on this chill, starry night!

A Blossoming Resolve

In a coat that's two sizes too big,
I stumbled through snow, looking quite rig.
My nose was red, my cheeks were too,
I found a snowman who laughed at my view.

The sun peeked through, oh what a sight,
I danced with delight, tried to take flight.
But my feet got stuck in a snowy embrace,
I wiggled and jiggled, then fell on my face.

With a chuckle I stood, a snowball in hand,
I flung it with glee, oh wasn't it grand?
The snowman replied, "Not quite the best aim!"
I shrugged and declared, "At least it's a game!"

So here in the snow, I found my own cheer,
Turning frosty mischief into joyful fear.
With each slip and slide, my spirit grew bright,
I flourished in laughter, a glorious sight.

Enduring the Winter's Grasp

Locked in the cabin, snug as a bug,
The ice outside gave my spirit a shrug.
Each snowflake that fell, a laugh from the sky,
While I searched for my mittens, oh me, oh my!

My neighbor's snow shovel looked like a spear,
He wielded it proudly, yet hid his own fear.
"I'll conquer the snow!" he exclaimed with a grin,
But fell on his back with a loud, squishy spin!

So we gathered our courage and boots to the door,
With snowmen in mind, we ventured for more.
We built them too big, with hats made of cheese,
All the world laughed at our snowy unease.

Frosty and silly, we twirled in the snow,
Who knew that the winter could put on such a show?
With giggles and joy, we danced in the cold,
Finding warmth in the laughter, worth more than gold.

Liberation from Chilling Shadows

The shadows grew long, and my toes became numb,
I plotted my escape with a low, rumbling thrum.
Donned in layers, like a burrito gone wrong,
Off I trundled, singing my favorite song.

Each step was a saga, a dance of the bold,
Jumping in puddles that shimmered like gold.
"Watch me, world!" I yelled with delight,
But fell on a patch that was slippery and white.

The icicles mocked while I lay in dismay,
Yet the sun peeked through, illuminating my play.
With a flick of my wrist, I tossed snow like confetti,
Declared myself the queen, all while feeling unsteady.

I gathered the sparkles, my crown made of frost,
Freed from the shadows, I laughed at the cost.
Winter might linger, but laughter it brings,
And I spun in circles, embracing its flings.

Rebirth in the Heat of Passion

As spring's teasing whispers replaced winter's hum,
I emerged in my glory, a bold little plum.
My cheeks were now rosy, my smile a bright sun,
Hello, world! It's time for some fun!

With shovels and rakes, my friends joined the fest,
We dug up the treasures that laid down to rest.
A flower! A leaf! Oh, what a surprise!
We laughed at the chill, we'd all paid our price.

The snowmen looked shocked, abandoned in time,
"Wait, come back!" they cried, "This is our prime!"
But we danced around them, the laughter resounded,
In the warmth of the sun, my spirit astounded.

So here's to the thaw, and the friends we hold dear,
With glee in our hearts, and nothing to fear.
The winter may return, with its chilling embrace,
But we'll summon our laughter, and joy will replace.

Milton Keynes UK
Ingram Content Group UK Ltd.
UKHW022342171124
451242UK00007B/108

9 789916 942963